T0132072

ABC's of Adoption

through the looking glass of the Bible

Written & Illustrated by
Sherri Jo Gallagher

WestBow Press books may be ordered through booksellers or by contacting:

WestBow Press
A Division of Thomas Nelson & Zondervan
1663 Liberty Drive
Bloomington, IN 47403
www.westbowpress.com
1 (866) 928-1240

Scripture quotations are taken from The Holy Bible, English Standard Version® (ESV®), Copyright © 2001 by Crossway, a publishing ministry of Good News Publishers. All rights reserved.

ISBN: 978-1-9736-6266-2 (sc)
ISBN: 978-1-9736-6267-9 (e)

Library of Congress Control Number: 2019906563

Print information available on the last page.

WestBow Press rev. date: 6/5/2019

WestBow
PRESS®
A DIVISION OF THOMAS NELSON
& ZONDERVAN

My beautiful child,
You make my world a brighter place.
You never cease to amaze me.
I am so proud of you
and love you with all that is in me!

My prayer for you is that you
know how loved you truly are.
Not just by your family,
but by our Creator who
knows the number of hairs on your head.
He shared His Son with us
so that we may believe and be
adopted into His loving arms forever.

family

Family becomes family

through many different ways.

ADOPTION brought you and I together...

and for this I shout

HOORAY!

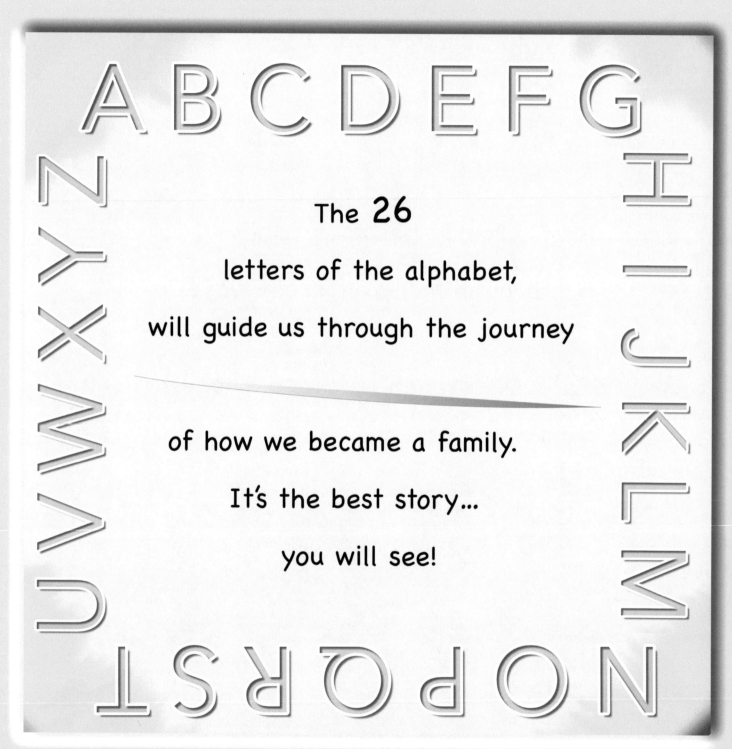

A B C D E F G H I J K L M N O P Q R S T U V W X Y Z

The **26**

letters of the alphabet,

will guide us through the journey

of how we became a family.

It's the best story...

you will see!

We prayed for you every day

humbly on bended knee.

God heard our prayer and answered it.

What an adventure this will BE!!

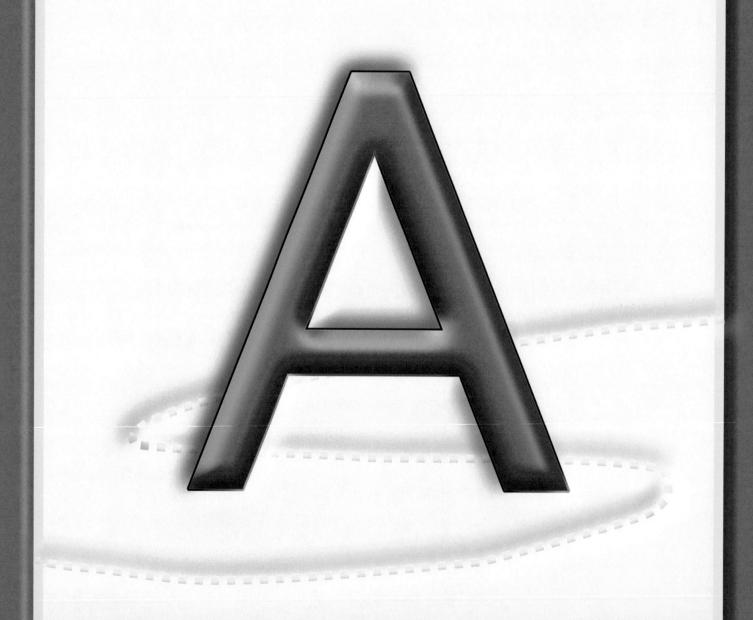

Starting at the beginning...

the very best place to start.

A is for <u>ADOPTION,</u>

which means we became family

first in our hearts!

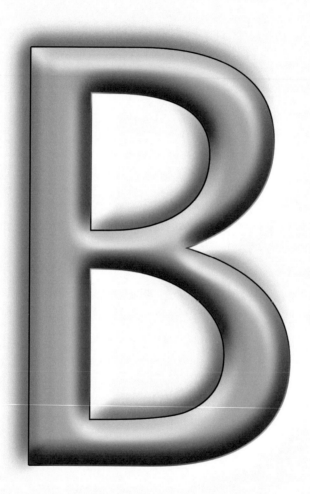

Next comes the letter B,

which stands for <u>BELIEVE</u>.

We believe that God has a

perfect plan,

which led YOU to ME!

For I
know the
plans I
have
for you.

Jeremiah
29:11

C is for <u>CREATION</u>.

God created the earth, the skies, the seas.

He isn't done yet though.

He still has time for you and me!

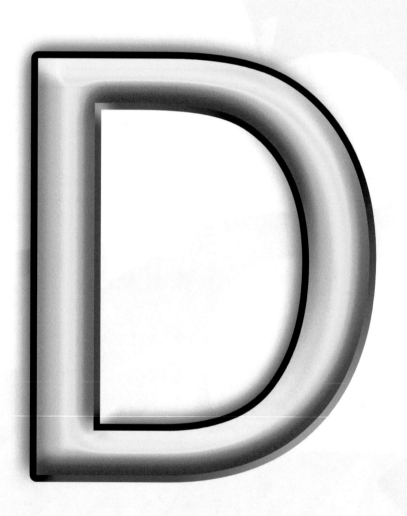

D stands for Jesus' <u>DEATH</u>

upon the cross...

so He can adopt ALL of us

as sons and daughters...

and not one of us be lost.

E

E stands for <u>ETERNAL LIFE</u>

for those who believe.

Jesus died and rose again.

This sacrifice has set us free!

F is for our FAMILY,

so important indeed.

God planned us before time began...

He knows exactly what we need.

I needed you and you needed me...

so He made us FAMILY.

G is for GROWING.

Growing in our bodies

and growing in our minds.

This family will grow in love,

even if we have different

skin, hair, or eyes.

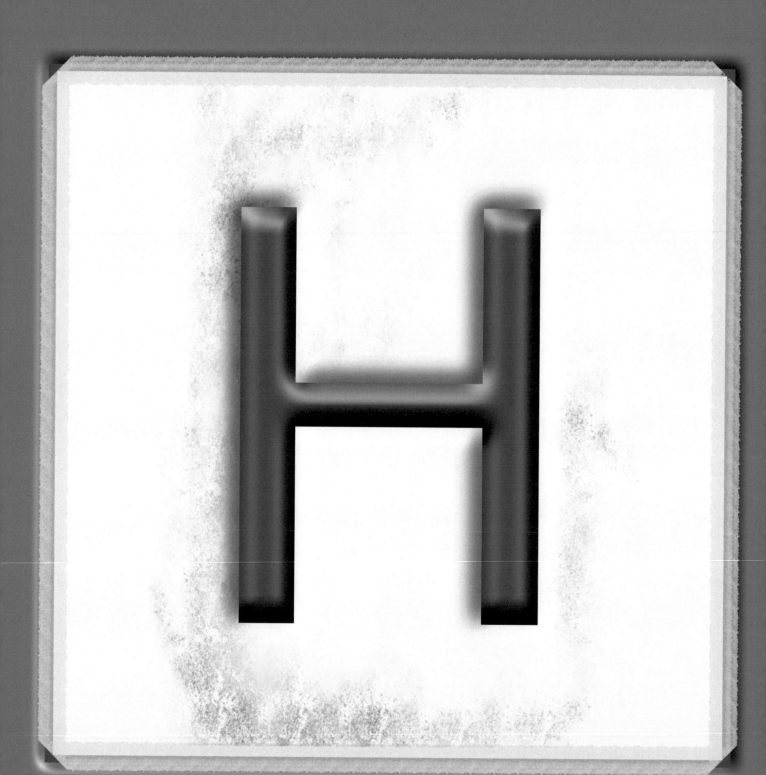

The letter H stands for

HEART and HOME.

So many obstacles

we have overcome.

We will share a heart just as we share a home.

I promise to love you

for all time to come.

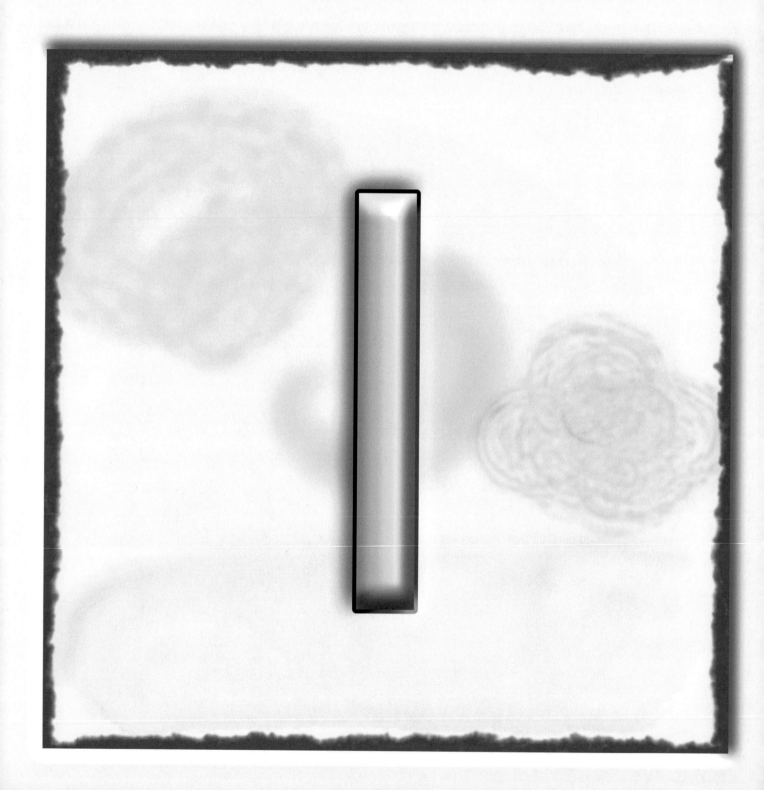

I says you are

<u>IMPORTANT</u>,

I am yours and you are mine.

Nothing will come between us –

not distance, place or time.

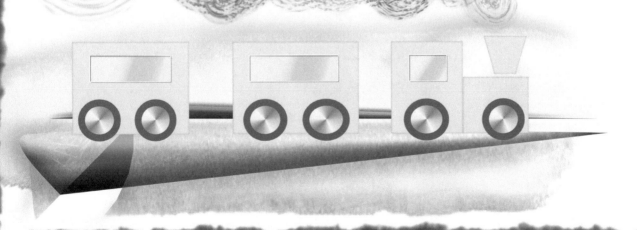

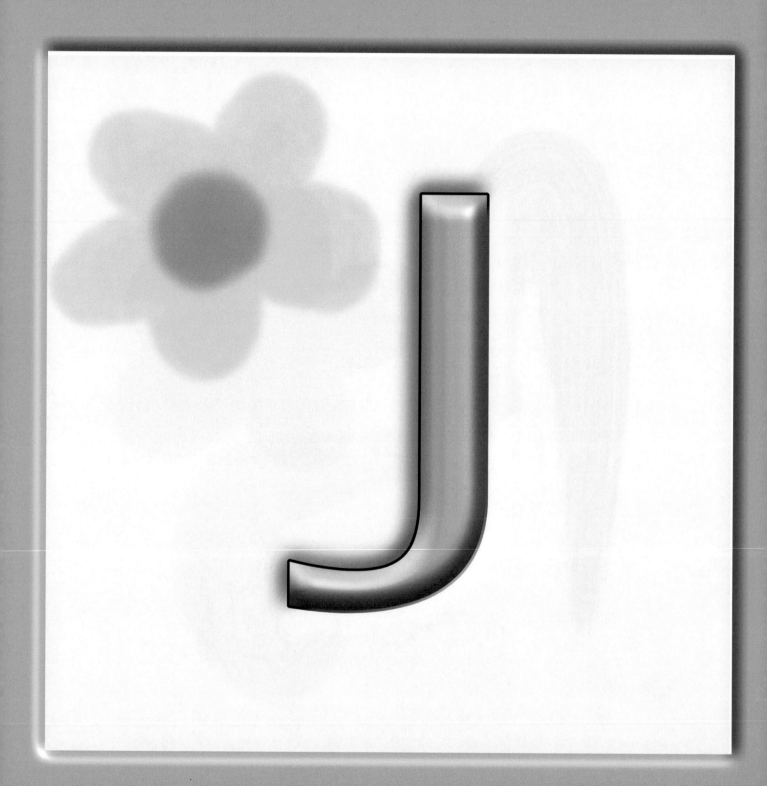

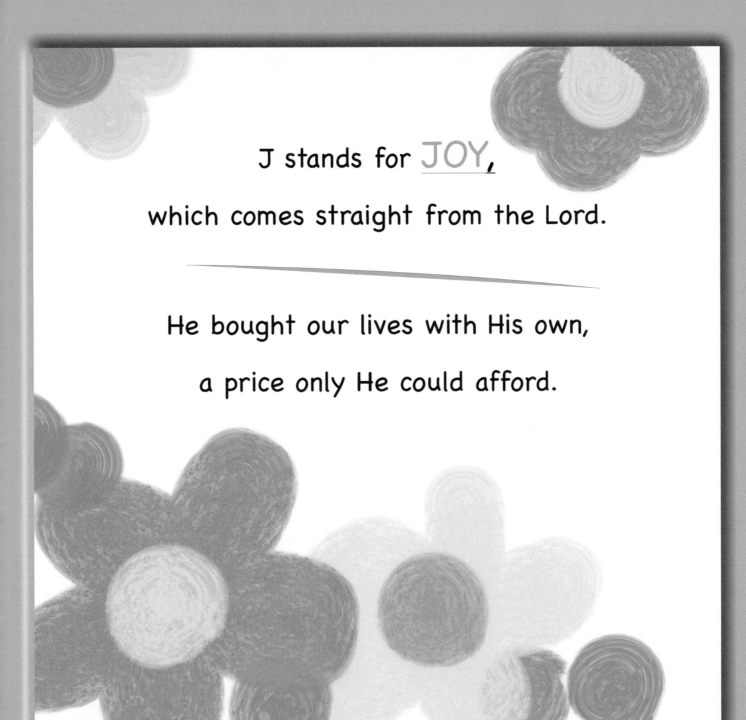

J stands for JOY,

which comes straight from the Lord.

He bought our lives with His own,

a price only He could afford.

K is for KINDNESS.

It's a word that should define us.

Share GOD'S love and compassion with everyone.

God gave us His Word to remind us.

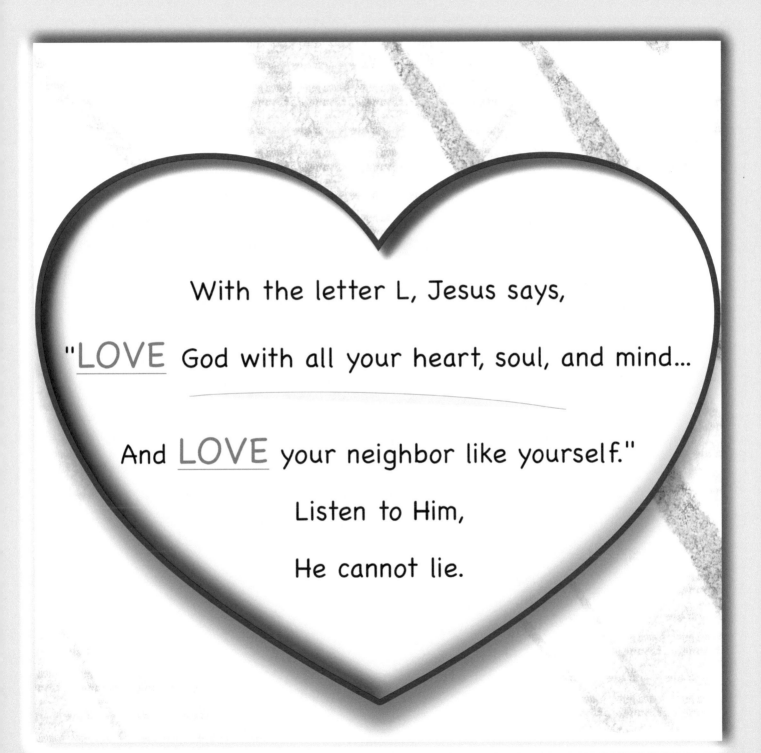

With the letter L, Jesus says,

"LOVE God with all your heart, soul, and mind...

And LOVE your neighbor like yourself."

Listen to Him,

He cannot lie.

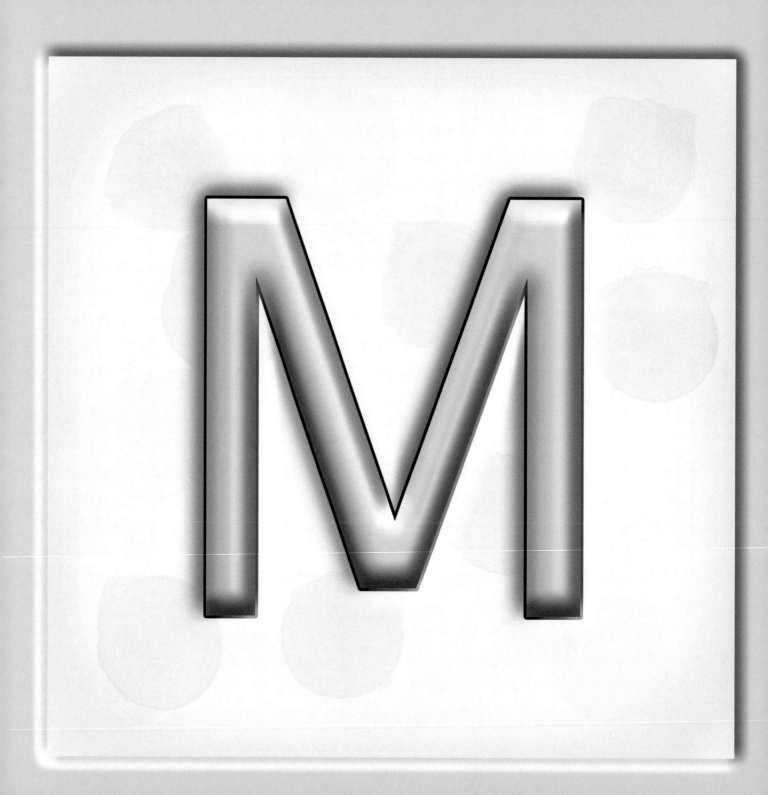

M is for MAMA,

this is a great thing you will see.

You needed a mother and the love of a family.

This part is important...

hold your ears and lean in close.

The special secret you must know...

is that your mama

needed YOU the most!

N is for <u>NIGHTTIME</u>,

when things may seem

more scary...

Don't worry, I'LL be here with you,

even if you are weary.

I will hold your hand,

just as you hold

my heart,

and the darkness

cannot tarry.

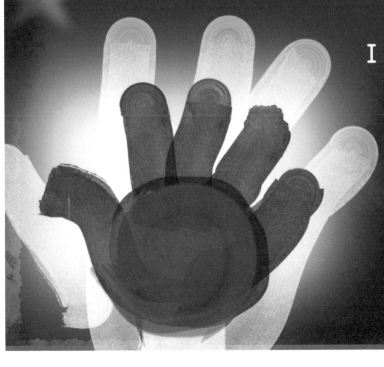

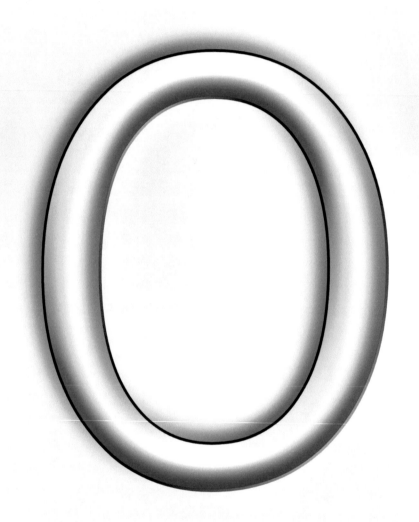

O is all about our **ONE** True God.

The Father, Son, and Holy Spirit.

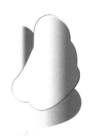

Let's share His love throughout the world and to all who live in it.

P is my for my PROMISE,

to love you through it all.

I will be here for you.

I will stand for you,

even when you fall.

Next comes the
letter Q.

I know there will

be QUESTIONS...

I will answer them as best I can
and the truth
is my intention.

R is a special letter
you can be certain.

When Jesus died for us,
God tore the temple curtain.

Through Jesus' blood
we have been REDEEMED.

We have a Savior who loves us.

My child, we have been set free!

Salvation is free to all who believe,
even though we don't deserve it.

We will enter into the joy of the Lord hearing,

"Well done, my

good and

faithful

SERVANT."

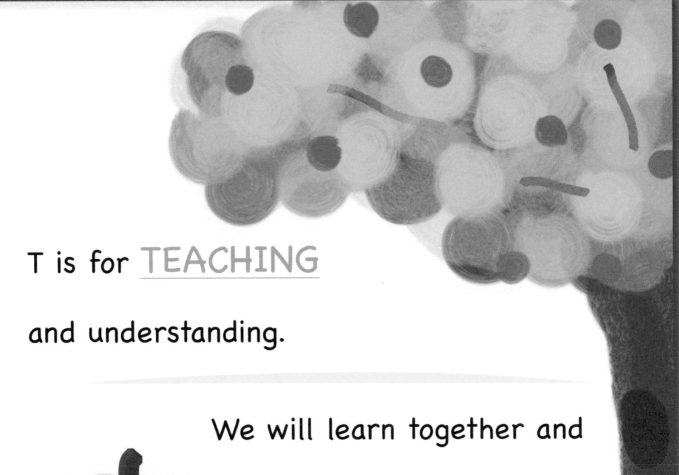

T is for TEACHING

and understanding.

We will learn together and
trust each other.
I will be a safe place
for you to land in.

U is SO GREAT because it stands for US!

You and me... we make a team.

Everything else is just a plus!

V stands for <u>VOYAGE</u>.

What a journey we are on!

Let's set sail on this pirate ship,

and see what adventures

come along!

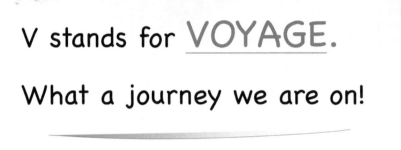

W is for the great big <u>WORLD</u> we live in.
It seems so big and yet so small.
We are all God's precious children.

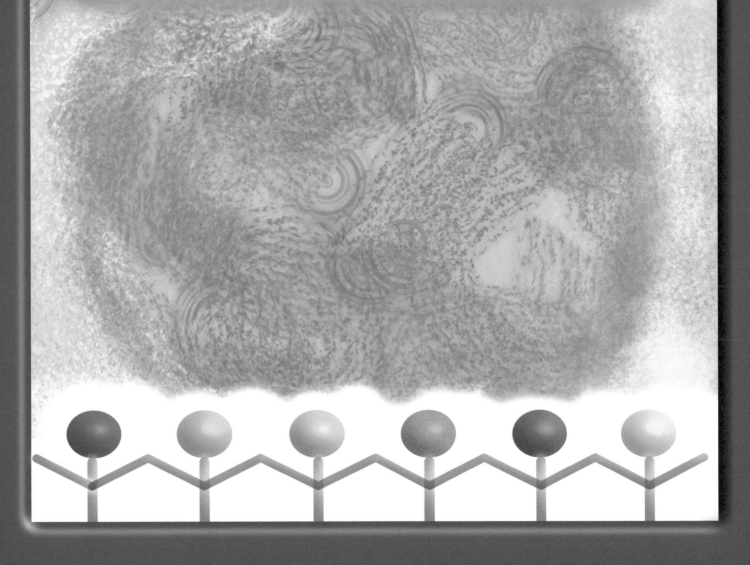

X marks the dotted line

on the paperwork we signed.

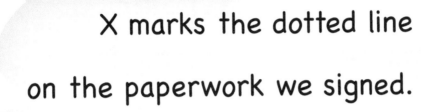

We loved you from the very start,

adoption is God's

GREAT DESIGN!

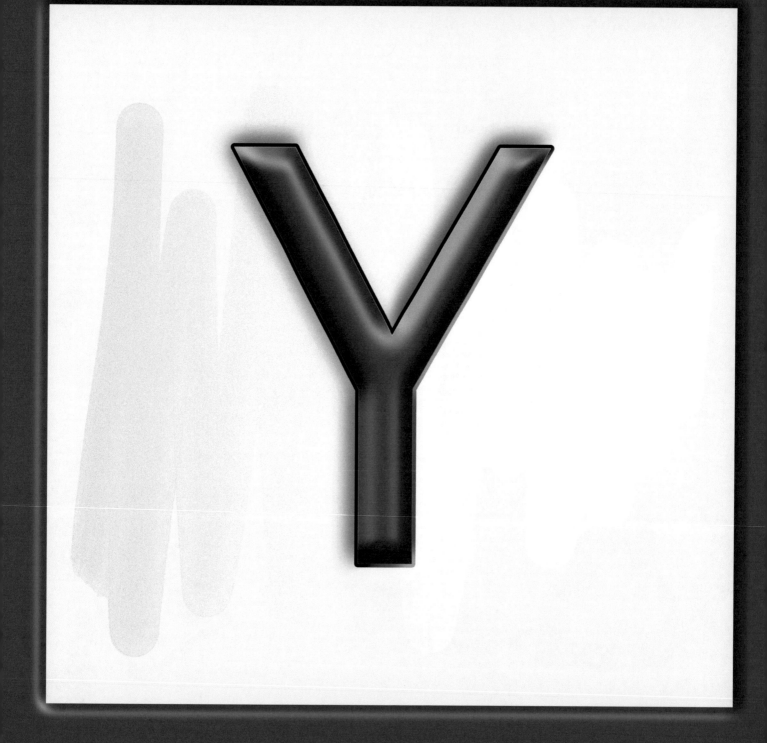

We are nearing the end of this book,

and I hope you have paid attention.

You are important and you are special.

This Y is all about <u>YOU</u>, no question!

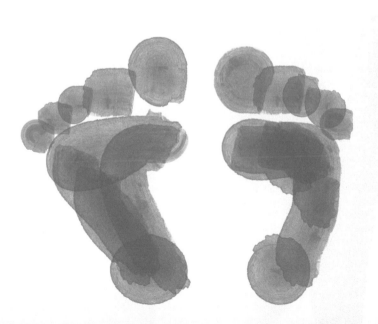

This is the last letter...

the Z stands for <u>ZERO</u>.

Zero time between

then and now,

I love you

my sweet child...

YOU ARE MY HERO!

I see that we have come

to the end of the alphabet.

Don't worry, our story isn't over yet.

As one story ends, another one begins...

We will write our own poem

with every day that we live.

So buckle up and hold on tight,

this story is all about YOU kid!

About the Author

Sherri Jo Gallagher grew up in Prescott, Arizona, before enlisting in the United States Army. After an exciting 11 years of service, she followed God's call to become a mother. She wants to help educate others about God's beautiful plan of adoption, as well as share God's love and truth with everyone she can (when she's not wrangling dogs and tiny humans).

Printed in the United States
By Bookmasters